SPACE DOG

Anthony Masters

Illustrated by
David Kearney

OXFORD
UNIVERSITY PRESS

Contents

1 NO ENTRY

11 July 2101

The strangest thing happened today. We've been at summer camp on Earth and are travelling back in the *Moonbeam* space shuttle to Moon Base. At breakfast, Captain Edwards' voice came over the loud speaker.

"Attention, please," she said. "We are about to pick up an unidentified object. We found it floating in space. In a few minutes we will be locking on and you'll notice a difference in the sound of our engines. The object will be taken to the cargo bay where it will be examined. I apologize to our passengers for any delay."

"I know where the cargo bay is," whispered my younger brother, Jack. "Let's go and have a look."

Gary, Jack's best mate, looked keen. "Are you coming with us, Dawn?" he asked.

I hesitated. I knew that we should be on our best behaviour as we were travelling without our parents. But I was curious, too. I guess I'm like my parents. They're scientists and they say scientists are always curious. So I went with the boys to the cargo bay. Jack led the way.

"It's next to the games room, so if anyone asks, pretend that's where we're going," whispered Jack.

Just before we got to the games room, Jack pointed to a half-open steel door. It was marked "CARGO BAY. NO ENTRY" in large red letters. We went in. The bay was full of moon buggies, crates and all sorts of remote-control vehicles.

Captain Edwards and her Security Chief were there, looking at something.

We crouched behind a large buggy. We could see that the mysterious object was already on board. It lay on the floor. It looked like a very large, furry glove.

Suddenly, something slid out of the furry glove. It seemed to be another, smaller, furry glove. Then, a small animal padded out, looking sleepy.

"A dog!" gasped Jack. I glared at him. We had to keep quiet. If we were found, we'd be in big trouble.

Luckily, Captain Edwards had spoken at the same time as Jack, so she hadn't heard him.

"A dog! Now why would a dog be floating in space?" she wondered out loud.

"There's a collar round his neck," said the Security Chief. He bent down to look more closely. "The name tag says he's called Hunter."

"Take him down to the sick bay," ordered Captain Edwards. "Ask the doctor to examine him. It's a pity we don't have a vet on board!"

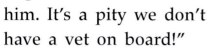

The Security Chief bent down to pick up the dog.

"Wait a minute," said the Captain, looking more closely at Hunter. "He's covered in fleas."

"They're too big to be fleas," replied the Security Chief.

Suddenly, a cloud of buzzing insects flew out of Hunter's fur.

"And fleas don't have wings!" said Captain Edwards, ducking as the creatures buzzed around in the cargo bay.

"Watch out!" I whispered. "Keep your heads down."

But it was too late. One of the creatures dived down into Gary's hair. I caught a glimpse of the insect's bulging eyes in a furry head, and its glowing purple body.

"Ow!" yelled Gary. "It's bitten me!"

The game was up. Captain Edwards stormed over to us. She looked furious.

"What are you doing in here?" she demanded.

We stood up. Gary scratched his head. He was more concerned about his bite than the captain's anger.

"One of those insects is caught in my hair," he said.

Captain Edwards looked concerned.

"Take this boy and the dog to the doctor," she told her Security Chief. "I want a medical report immediately."

Gary left with the Security Chief and Hunter. Captain Edwards turned to us.

"I'm very disappointed in you," she said. "I expect all orders on *Moonbeam* to be followed."

"I'm sorry, Captain Edwards," I said. "It won't happen again."

"Well, it had better not," said Captain Edwards. Then she looked thoughtful.

"I've had a report that a dog vanished last week from a craft coming back from deep space," she said. "I wonder if it was Hunter. The word 'kidnapped' was used, but who would want to kidnap a dog, and why?"

I can't sleep, so I'm writing down what happened in my diary, trying to make some sense of it.

2   Aliens on board

12 July 2101

When I woke up, Jack was sitting on the end of my bed.

"Let's go and see Gary," he urged.

"Are we allowed to?" I asked.

"I don't know," said Jack. "I'm worried about him, and I'm going to see him anyway. You don't have to come."

"I'll come," I replied quickly. I wanted to be with Jack so he would stay out of trouble.

We were having a quick breakfast when Captain Edwards made an announcement. "Good morning, everyone. I would like to inform you that the space capsule we took on board yesterday contained a dog. The dog is infested with unknown winged insects."

"Unfortunately, one of our passengers has been bitten and we are keeping him in the sick bay. Please remember that some areas of the shuttle are for crew only. This is in the interests of everyone's safety."

Jack and I swapped guilty looks.

After breakfast, Jack said, "I'm still going to the sick bay. I'm worried about Gary."

I nodded. We had to find out what these insects were and what had happened to Gary.

When we arrived, the nurse was looking worried.

"We've come to see Gary," I explained. "Is that insect still in his hair?"

"Yes," she said. "The doctor was going to try to remove it this morning, but Gary's disappeared."

Just then, Gary walked in. He was wearing his pyjamas, but he now looked very odd. He was staring ahead with a strange fixed look in his eyes. His eyes, usually a greeny brown, now looked black.

"Where have you been?" asked the nurse. "I've been looking for you everywhere."

Gary didn't reply. He just stared ahead.

"Tell me where you've been, Gary," repeated the nurse.

But Gary climbed back into bed without speaking. I had this weird idea that somehow he'd been switched off. The nurse tucked him into bed.

"Gary!" I hissed, but he lay back and closed his eyes.

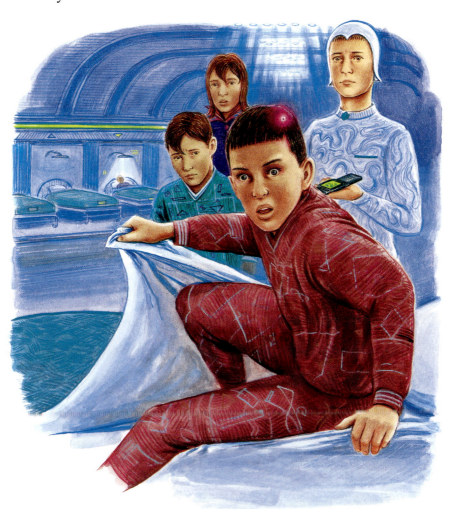

"Now, leave him alone," instructed the nurse. She was looking worried. I think she knew something was wrong.

"Did you notice the colour of his eyes?" I asked. "Maybe the insects have taken him over!"

"What?" Jack looked surprised.

"Suppose the insects are really alien creatures," I said, my mind racing now. "Suppose they stole Hunter . . . "

"What nonsense!" interrupted the nurse.

". . . and took him to that weird furry glove thing," I said.

"It was odd that the glove – their capsule – was in *Moonbeam*'s flight path," said Jack.

"Yes, it's as if they wanted to be picked up," I said slowly.

"Let's go and speak to Captain Edwards," said Jack.

3   In the cockpit

We knocked on the door of the cockpit. It was opened by the Second Officer.

"What do you two want?" He didn't seem friendly. "Only crew are allowed in the cockpit."

"We've got something important to tell Captain Edwards," I said.

The officer sighed. "If this is some kind of joke . . ."

"It's not," said Jack firmly.

The cockpit was packed with computers, monitors and control panels. It also had an amazing view of the galaxy – it looked like a black cloth sprinkled with diamonds. Captain Edwards was studying a map of the solar system.

"How can I help you?" she asked a little impatiently.

I began nervously.

"Gary went missing from the sick bay. Now he's back in bed and keeps staring ahead without speaking. His eyes have gone black."

The captain frowned.

"Suppose those insects in Hunter's fur are aliens," suggested Jack boldly. "They might be planning to take over *Moonbeam*."

"And suppose I'm President of the United States!" replied Captain Edwards sarcastically. "Is that all you've come to tell me?"

"We wondered whether you had found out anything about those insect creatures?" I said.

"I'm sure our medical team have the problem in hand," snapped Captain Edwards. "Now, please excuse me, I have work to do."

I'm in bed now and writing up my diary. I've tried to sleep but I can't stop thinking about those weird insects. They scare me, but I don't know why.

4 Setting the trap

13 July 2101

I slept badly last night, dreaming the insects were tangled up in my own hair. Looking into a dream mirror, I saw my eyes had turned black.

Then I heard a knock at the door and I struggled out of sleep.

"Who is it?" I called.

"Only me." Jack came in and sat down on the edge of my bed. "We've got to see Gary today, whatever the nurse says."

I agreed. Half an hour later we were outside the sick bay. We opened the door, hoping we could see Gary before the nurse saw us.

"There's no one here," began Jack, but I put my fingers to my lips. I could hear whispering. Or was it whispering? It was more like buzzing.

It was getting louder and more threatening. Jack could hear it, too. It sounded different to anything I had ever heard before – an alien sound.

"Quick, in here!" hissed Jack, pulling me into the laundry room. We were just in time. Seconds later, as we were peering out of the small window in the door, we saw a group of people walking past.

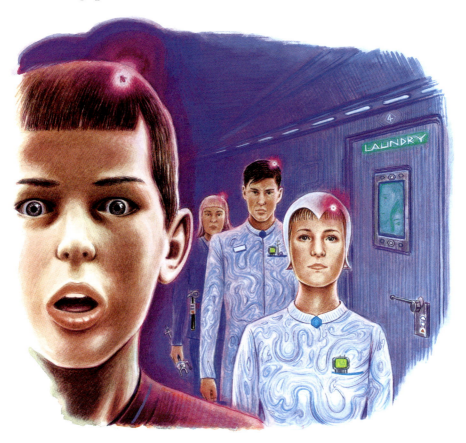

There was Gary, the nurse, a doctor and one of the shuttle's engineers. They were all staring ahead. Their eyes were black. They walked like zombies, and all of them were making a strange buzzing sound.

"They must be under alien power," whispered Jack. "But what are they going to do?"

I said nothing. I was too scared. Were the aliens going to try to take over the shuttle?

Suddenly, we heard a loud bark and Hunter came padding down the corridor. His eyes were black, too. There were dozens of the insects in his fur. Hunter began to scratch at the laundry-room door. Jack and I froze with fear. Finally, Hunter gave up and trotted off down the corridor. Then there was silence.

"I bet Hunter will come back now he knows we're here. What are we going to do?" I whispered. "We've got to tell someone."

"Captain Edwards won't listen," said Jack. "We'll have to think of something else."

Then I had an idea.

"Come on, Jack, follow me."

I led Jack out of the laundry room. We walked down the corridor and through a door marked "SUPPLIES".

"We need a vacuum cleaner," I said, scanning the shelves.

"A what?" asked Jack, looking at me as if I'd gone crazy.

"A vacuum cleaner," I said again. "If we can get Hunter on his own, we could clean those creatures out of his fur."

"Good thinking!" Jack grinned. "Look, over there."

We pulled a vacuum cleaner off a shelf. I found a power point and plugged it in.

"Wait a minute," said Jack. "If those insects really *are* aliens, they won't let themselves get caught. They must have brains – of a kind."

"We'll just have to hope that they don't know much about our world. They might not know what a vacuum cleaner is."

Jack nodded uneasily. "But how can we get Hunter here for us to clean him?"

That was another problem. I thought I had come up with a brilliant idea, but I couldn't think of an answer to this question.

"Wait a minute," said Jack, and he began to search along the shelves again. With a cry of triumph, Jack pulled out a packet of biscuits.

"I think Hunter might go for these."

"I don't think the aliens will," I said doubtfully.

"Don't be daft. We'll trap Hunter with the biscuits. While he's scoffing them, you can grab him and wrap him in your jacket. Then we can poke the nozzle of the cleaner underneath it."

Would our plan work? It would have to – it was all we had and we could hear that strange buzzing sound again, getting nearer.

Jack crept into the corridor. He unwrapped the packet of biscuits and quickly scattered some of them on the floor.

"Wait till I give you a signal," he hissed, "and then grab Hunter."

Panic swept over me. I seemed to have ended up with the worst job.

"You'll have to help," I whispered, taking off my jacket.

Suddenly, Hunter appeared. When he saw the trail of biscuits, he put his head down and began to swallow them whole. After a while he choked, then began to eat more slowly.

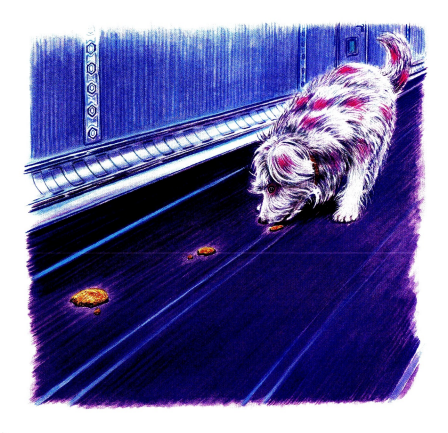

5 Capture!

So far so good, I thought. Hunter was following the trail of biscuits, but there was an angry buzzing coming from his fur. I thought the aliens might be getting suspicious. There was no time to lose.

"Let's go for it!" Jack whispered. We began to walk slowly towards Hunter. I held my jacket in my hand and Jack clutched our secret weapon, the vacuum cleaner. Silently, we got to Hunter.

I looked at Jack. One wrong move and the insects might attack us.

"Now!" shouted Jack. I dived at Hunter, smothering him in my jacket. He struggled and the buzzing sound grew more frantic, but it was soon drowned out by the noise of the vacuum cleaner.

Jack buried the nozzle in Hunter's fur. We could hear the insects rattling through the nozzle and into the vacuum cleaner. Soon Hunter relaxed. I carefully took my jacket off him. His coat looked clean. Jack switched off the cleaner.

"I think Hunter's glad to get rid of them," I said.

Jack nodded. "I reckon they just took him over," he said. "They dognapped him!"

We grinned at each other, feeling like we'd won. But then we heard a buzzing noise coming from the vacuum cleaner. It was growing louder by the second. I stared down at it. The battle wasn't over yet.

"What shall we do with them now?" said Jack. I didn't know. My plan hadn't got that far. I looked around desperately. Then I spotted the freezer.

"What about shoving them in there?" I said.

"Good idea," replied Jack.

"Can you get the bag off the vacuum cleaner without letting any of them out?" I asked him. "I'll open the freezer."

Jack nodded. My panic grew as the buzzing got louder.

"We'll do a
countdown," I said,
trying to stay calm.
"On the count of one,
you open the cleaner
and grab the bag. On
the count of two, you shove
it in the freezer. On the count of three,
I slam the door shut. Ready?"

"Ready," said Jack. I noticed his hands were shaking.

"One!"

Jack opened the vacuum cleaner and grabbed the bag. He tried to pull it out but it seemed to be stuck.

"Hurry up!" I hissed.

"What do you think I'm trying to do?" snapped Jack. He was trembling all over now. Then, suddenly, the bag came free and he almost fell back.

"Two! Get the bag in the freezer."

Jack dashed over, his hands clasped tightly round the neck of the bag. The buzzing sound got even louder as the aliens fought to get out. But Jack managed to ram the bag deep into the freezer before they could escape.

"And three!" I yelled as I slammed the freezer door shut and we both stood gasping.

We'd done it!

6 The battle goes on

Hunter nuzzled my legs. I gave him a pat and he lay down and closed his eyes. Jack pulled out the last biscuit and held it under Hunter's nose. The little dog opened his eyes. They were no longer a glaring black, but a soft brown. Hunter licked Jack's hand and munched the last biscuit.

"We still don't really know what the aliens want," said Jack. "My guess is that they want to take over human beings, control their minds. That's what they seem to have been doing so far."

He broke off, staring at four figures who had appeared in the doorway. A wave of fear swept over me. We'd got rid of the aliens in Hunter's fur, but what about the insect in Gary's hair? I glanced at the heads of the nurse, doctor and engineer. Yes, there was movement there, too, and that strange buzzing sound. All four people were staring ahead, their eyes black.

"Do you think they can see us?" I said as we flattened ourselves against the wall by the freezer.

"I don't know," whispered Jack. "Maybe they can't see us, but I think they can sense us."

The buzzing got louder. Gary and the others walked towards our hiding place. I held my breath. Then, without warning, the shuttle began to roll, sending us all spinning.

"Oh no! They've done something to the ship!" cried Jack as we were flung into the centre of the room.

We landed in front of the group. The *Moonbeam* stopped rolling.

Gary began to speak in a zombie-like voice, **"Where are the others? We sense they are trapped. You must let them go. The shuttle will not function unless our comrades are released."**

"Who are you?" asked Jack.

"We are Zitons from Planet Zitax. Our sun is dying and we must find a new world."

Although I was scared, I was curious, too.

"What's your world like?" I asked.

"Look into our eyes," said Gary.

Slowly, each group member's eyes grew until they were enormous. When we looked into them we saw a strange world that looked like a jungle of grey fur. Hundreds of insect-like aliens climbed and crawled through the jungle. I realized that this alien world looked exactly like Hunter's fur.

Then Gary went on, **"We need a new planet. Your Earth is suitable. Do not stand in our way."**

The Zitons' threat was now perfectly clear. We had to think quickly.

"If you want to see where your comrades are, come with us," I said.

"Dawn, no!" shouted Jack. "Don't show them . . ." but Gary and his three companions were following me to the freezer.

7 Winners or losers?

Hunter heard the anger in Jack's voice. He stood in front of the freezer and began to growl. A couple of Zitons hovered over him.

"Get out of the way, Hunter," I urged. Instead, Hunter began to bark bravely. One of the Zitons took a dive at him, but Hunter was too quick for it.

"Dawn, don't!" shouted Jack again. He didn't understand my plan. Did he think I'd been taken over, too? I noticed one of the Zitons was buzzing over *his* head. I had to distract them or it would be too late.

"They want to find their friends," I said, "and so they shall." I whipped open the door of the freezer and the Zitons dived in. I slammed it shut again.

"We've got the lot!" I yelled in triumph.

"Brilliant!" said Jack, impressed. "For a horrible moment, I thought you'd been taken over, too!"

I grinned. "It was all part of the plan!" I said.

We looked through the glass door of the freezer. The vacuum bag was almost frozen. Icicles were already forming on the wings of the Zitons we could see.

"We must make sure that they're kept frozen," I said. "Then they can be examined properly."

"What am I doing here?" asked a familiar voice. We turned to see Gary and the others looking around as if they had just woken up.

"It's a long story," said Jack. "Come with us to see Captain Edwards and you'll hear exactly what happened."

"I'm sorry I didn't believe you," said Captain Edwards when she saw us in the cockpit half an hour later. "But we do need to keep quiet about all this."

"Why?" asked Jack. "These Zitons are dangerous. People should know about them."

Captain Edwards scratched her head and hurried on. "I don't want to worry the other passengers." She cleared her throat uneasily. "Everything is under control now, so please keep what's happened to yourselves."

"But what if we didn't catch all the Zitons?" I began.

"Look, I'm the captain of this ship and I issue orders," said Captain Edwards sternly. "You have already disobeyed me once and if you do so again you'll be in serious trouble with Security." Her voice seemed dull and forced.

"Yes, Captain," said Jack. He took my arm. "Come on, Dawn, let's go."

Jack, Gary and I walked back to our cabins.

"It's no use arguing with her," said Jack. "It's her ship. Anyway, it's all over now. I can't wait to tell Mum and Dad about this adventure."

But I was uneasy. Had I imagined it, or had Captain Edwards' eyes always been that dark?

14 July 2101

I've just read what I wrote yesterday. Jack's right, of course. We've got to trust Captain Edwards. My imagination just runs away with me sometimes. At least we have a great story to tell everyone when we get back to Moon Base. Maybe the newspapers will want to publish my account of the Battle against the Zitons!

There's a buzzing noise in my cabin. I think there must be a problem with one of the power units. I've told the engineer, but he's not come yet. That's odd – it seems to be getting louder. I hope it's not . . .